A celebration of friendship

You're the Best

the Satellite Sisters

Also by the Satellite Sisters

Satellite Sisters' UnCommon Senses

Also by Lian Dolan

Helen of Pasadena
Elizabeth the First Wife

You're the Best

a celebration of friendship

PROSPECT
·PARK·
BOOKS

Published by Prospect Park Books
2359 Lincoln Avenue
Altadena, CA 91001
www.prospectparkbooks.com

Library of Congress Cataloging-in-Publication Data

You're the best : a celebration of friendship / the Satellite Sisters. -- First edition.
        pages cm
1. Friendship--Humor. 2. Female friendship--Humor. I. Satellite Sisters (Radio program)
PN6231.F748Y68 2015
818'.602--dc23
                                2015018988

Cover design & illustrations by Nancy Nimoy
Page design & layout by Amy Inouye, Future Studio

Learn more about the Satellite Sisters at www.satellitesisters.com.

To our Satellite Sisters (and Misters) around the world.
You're the best.

To Begin

Satellite Sisters has always been about the sound of friendship. When friends get together, there's laughter and storytelling, disclosure and advice, headlines and hair talk, tears and hugs, then more laughter. For us, the support of our female friends has been a constant source of sustenance in our lives, so it's a natural topic for us to tackle in print. *You're the Best: A Celebration of Friendship* is our thank-you note for those relationships: a chance for gratitude, grace, and, of course, more laughter.

We five Dolan sisters have been writing and talking about this topic for years, but for this book we wanted to invite the Next Generation of Satellite Sisters—our nieces, daughters, and daughters-in-law—to share their stories and lessons. So we're grateful to Next Gens Ruthie, Meghan, Katherine, Lauren, Vera, and Fiona. Between them and the five of us, you'll find voices from fifteen to sixty chiming in with essays, lists, texts, even a Mad Lib. It's been a pleasure to put together. The good news is that no matter how the communication methods have changed, the importance of our friends—the people who get us up, get us going, and get us through—has not.

Thank you, friends. #ytb

Julie Dolan   Sheila Dolan   Lian Dolan
Liz Dolan   Monica Dolan

Family

Play

Change

The Last Word

The Next Generation

Thank Yous

About the Satellite Sisters

Julie Dolan, the oldest sister, is the foreign correspondent. She has lived and worked in Moscow and Bangkok, and while she and her husband now live in the foreign land of Dallas, Texas, she continues to travel extensively, bringing her observations back to the Satellite Sisters. (Recent adventures have included "girlfriend trips" to North Korea and Uzbekistan.) Before moving abroad, Julie worked at and taught in a number of leading U.S. universities and business schools, including UCLA, Stanford, and Tulane. She has a degree in government from Smith College and an MBA from Penn State. She and her husband have two adult sons, two great daughters-in-law, and four grandchildren. Her motto: You're never too old to make new friends. She didn't plan to live in State College, New Orleans, Los Angeles, San Francisco, Bangkok, Moscow, or Dallas, but everywhere she landed, someone was waiting with an open heart. Julie is grateful to the friends near and far who invited her for coffee, let her join the team, or thought she might like their book club. They're the best.

Liz Dolan, the second oldest sister, is the chief marketing officer for Fox International Channels in Los Angeles, a job that means she is rarely actually in Los Angeles. Liz has been known to record, edit, and post a weekend edition of the Satellite Sisters podcast from her laptop while sitting on a bed in an Istanbul hotel. Before creating Satellite Sisters, she was the vice president of global marketing at NIKE, where she worked for a decade, and CMO of the Oprah Winfrey Network. She has twice been named Woman of the Year in the sports business, called a "Woman to Watch" by *Adweek*, and named one of the Most Powerful Women in Cable. Her friends might describe her as "devoted but rarely available." They frequently enjoy staying in her sunny Santa Monica apartment even when she is not there. Liz has a degree in comparative literature from Brown University. Occasionally, she sneaks away to her bungalow in Bend, Oregon with her dog, Ferris.

Sheila Dolan, the middle sister, teaches third grade in Los Angeles. A Hunter College graduate with two master's degrees in teaching, she has worked both in the classroom and on the administration side in both public and private schools from Manhattan to L.A. Her philosophy of teaching is simple: Every child can learn, just not on the same day. Sheila is also a two-time individual Gracie Allen award-winner for comedy as the Satellite Sisters' self-styled entertainment reporter, Entertaining Sheila. Her natural ability to laugh at herself and tell funny stories comes in handy when faced with twenty-three nine-year-olds. Sheila's best friends haven't changed much since her twelfth birthday, when she locked her four closest partners-in-crime in her bedroom for a preteen angst session. She prefers deep, intimate conversations about life's injustices (involving her), the dwindling dating pool (from her perspective), and the joys of motherhood, takeout food, Ryan Gosling, and Bobbi Brown stick foundation. Single with an adult daughter, Sheila is a swimmer who once went on a strenuous hike.

Monica Dolan, the second youngest sister, has spent most of her career as hospital RN specializing in cardiac care. She has worked for more than two decades in intensive-care units and operating rooms while also working on studies for the approval of new medical devices. Currently she is a clinical research coordinator for acute stroke trials at a university hospital. Monica leads many of the health and wellness discussions on Satellite Sisters and also has her own segment entitled "Science of the Obvious." She has a BS from Georgetown, is single, and lives in Portland, Oregon. Monica embraces the damp Northwest lifestyle by going to the movies on Saturday afternoons, reading hardcover books from the library, and drinking coffee. She loves meeting her Pac NW friends for walks and dinner and cherishes her weekend getaways with her old college pals.

Lian Dolan, the youngest sister, is a writer, broadcaster, and the author of two novels: *Helen of Pasadena,* which spent more than a year on the *Los Angeles Times* bestseller list and was nominated as Best Fiction by the Southern California Independent Booksellers, and *Elizabeth the First Wife,* which landed on the *L.A. Times* bestseller list its first week out. Lian has been a columnist for *Working Mother, O, the Oprah Magazine,* and Oprah.com and is currently writing a column for *Pasadena Magazine* and working on her next novel. Lian created the Chaos Chronicles, a blog and weekly podcast about her life as a working mom that was developed by Nickelodeon as a half-hour sitcom. Her degree in classics from Pomona College did nothing to prepare her for all of this. Lian lives in Pasadena, California with her husband and their two sons. Her friends know that she is sketchy on photo holiday cards, mailing birthday gifts, and returning loaned books but strong on meal deliveries and paying for drinks. She has walked around the Rose Bowl with her friends approximately a million times in order to stay sane and stay in shape, with mixed results on both fronts.

Life

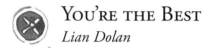 YOU'RE THE BEST
Lian Dolan

Hello, my friend…

Just a quick note to tell you how much I value our friendship. Too sincere? Maybe, but totally true.

I'll never forget the day I met you *in fourth grade/at summer camp/in health class/ at orientation/in the break room/in Mommy & Me/at law school/when the kids started kindergarten/on that hellish work trip.* My first thought was, "I wish I had her hair." My next thought was, "I hope she likes me."

And I'm so glad you did.

You are the type of person who keeps me sane, makes me laugh, and accepts me for who I am, which, let's face it, is not always a bundle of joy.

But you always seem glad to see me anyway, even if somehow way too much time has passed. We pick up where we left off, no problem.

You appreciate my love of *Jane Austen/Nora Roberts/Katniss Everdeen*, my obsession with *Whitney/Mariah/Beyoncé,* and my devotion *HGTV/ The West Wing/Law & Order.* The love we share for *Colin Firth/Justin Timberlake/Taye Diggs* is mutual, but I think if the occasion ever did arise where one of us could act upon it, you'd let me win, and I'm not sure I'm a big enough person to do the same for you.

You remember my birthday. You admire my creativity. You pick up the check when I least expect it. You tell me I look great even when I don't. And when I actually look great, you tell me I look fabulous.

You were there for me when I really needed a *gut check/amateur medical advice/intervention.* You listened to my symptoms and made your recommendations over the phone while simultaneously cooking dinner and Googling, which is a special skill. The fact that you can quote medical journals, *US Magazine*, and *Eat, Pray, Love* in your treatment plan is icing on the cake.

You were there for me when I *blew out my knee/went into pre-term*

labor/broke up with that idiot, and you never once chastised me for
over-reaching, doing too much, or trying too hard. All of which I was
guilty of, of course. But you came with tea and sympathy, aka wine and
parmesan crisps, and said exactly the right thing, which was nothing, and
just let me overanalyze the situation to death.

You were there for me when I got *fired/promoted/caught abusing the
shipping and receiving privileges at work* and you had the perfect advice,
which was, "Never cry at the office." You were so right, and I really
learned my lesson, maybe a tad too late that to save that one job, but
now, I'm solid. I've learned to cry in the car at lunch, and that's been a
real boost to my career.

You were there for me when I *got bangs/started my cat-centered business/
entered that karaoke contest* and managed not to blurt out, "You're crazy."
I could see you thought so, but you held your tongue and just asked,
"What can I do to help?" You might have tried a little harder to talk me
out of my bad idea, but no hard feelings.

You were there for me when I *had the third baby/got divorced/heard the
diagnosis* and I thought I might never leave the house again. You showed
up with your signature Caesar salad and you told me, in the nicest way,

"Take a shower, put on some makeup, and get it together, for God's sake."
Now that I think about it, you were kind of mean, but that was just what
I needed.

You were there for me when I lost *the pregnancy/my other great friend/
my mother,* and never once did you say, like so many others, "'It's for the
best." Because it wasn't for the best, not at all. One day I had somebody
in my life, and the next day I didn't. How could that be for the best? You
showed up and stayed the night. You brought soup and bread. You sent
that beautiful arrangement of all-white flowers with the roses, hydrangeas,
and stephanotis that was just perfect. And now, when I see white flowers,
I think of my loss and your kindness, and it's all right.

I owe you for that night at that dive bar on our road trip. I should not
line dance under the influence, and I think we both know that now.

I owe you for letting me borrow that really expensive evening clutch with
the feathers. I had no idea puppies were attracted to feathers.

I owe you for that really poor financial advice I gave to you. It was loud
on the subway, but I really thought I heard that guy in the suit say, "Buy
Enron."

I owe you for Brad. Let's not talk about him ever again.

You're smart. You're funny. You text just the right amount. You're the one person who tells me about the thing in my teeth without sounding just a little bit superior.

Thank you for the years.

Thank you for the dancing.

Thank you for the sunshine.

Thank you for encouragement.

Thank you for the empathy.

Thank you for the laughter.

Thank you for your friendship.

You're the best.

Xxoo

 What Is a Satellite Sister?

What exactly is a Satellite Sister? A Satellite Sister is a sounding board for your wacky career plans, a guaranteed huddle-in-the-corner partner at neighborhood parties, someone who's seen you in your glasses. A Satellite Sister brings information, perspective, and balance to your life when you are lacking all three. A Satellite Sister is the person who gets you through, makes you laugh, and, every once in awhile, changes your mind.

Interdependence gets a bad rap in this country, and we'd like to change that. We believe that self-sufficiency is overrated; we're all for relying on your people to make life a little more satisfying, interesting, and fun. There's nothing wrong with mixing a little commiseration in with the camaraderie. We all need someone to see us through life's travails, from an unfortunate haircut to an unfortunate marriage. People need people, as the song goes. And everyone needs a Satellite Sister.

Satellite Sisters come in individuals, pairs, or large groups. They can be female, male, single, married, straight, gay, or undecided. Some are older, some are younger, and some are just your age. They might be your actual sisters or cousins or aunts—or they might be completely unrelated: college roommates, best friends from grade school, or your training partners for the New York City Marathon. Whether they live next door or across the country, they are there for you. Your Satellite Sisters get you through life, one cup of coffee at a time.

What exactly is a Satellite Sister? A friend, of course, but more than that. She's the person you call when the best thing in your life happens. Or the worst. So please: Call your Satellite Sister.

When to Call Your Satellite Sister

When your one-hour layover becomes a five-hour layover.

When that guy from college friends you on Facebook and his status is Single.

When that guy from college friends you on Facebook and you see the photos of him, his lovely wife, and their three beautiful children.

When you need to decide between grad school and an unpaid internship.

When you're writing your resume and need to recast your skills as a waitress as something akin to a financial advisor.

When you discover the guy in the cubicle next to you is making $15,000 more for the same job.

When you're about to use this month's rent money on a down payment for next summer's vacation house.

When you've got a combination 8 a.m. presentation/babysitter no-show/
    vomiting child situation.

When your ex-husband's lawyer asks you out on a date right after you
    sign the divorce papers.

When you get transferred to San Francisco.

When corporate HQ moves to Trenton.

When you find a lump.

When the lump is benign.

When the lump isn't benign.

When your life big issue is cocktail dress vs. jumpsuit.

When your life big issue is stay vs. go.

When your smartass email response to one person gets sent company-
    wide.

When Mindy Kaling re-tweets you.

When you experience an unexplained dermatological situation.

When the dermatologist looks like George Clooney.

When you just want to talk about Kate Middleton's clothes.

When a text won't cut it.

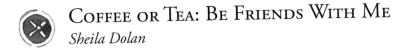

COFFEE OR TEA: BE FRIENDS WITH ME
Sheila Dolan

My love of coffee and affinity for coffee drinkers started back in high school. I don't think the nuns at Covent of the Sacred Heart realized that the arrival of a new beverage machine in the student lounge would kick off a lifetime obsession with caffeine and my defining rule of friendship. Coffee drinkers were my first best friends, and they still are.

We congregated around that old automatic coffee machine, which spit out just two varieties: black or with sugary powdered milk. Maybe it was a tiny rebellious streak we all shared as early as 1975, which manifested in drinking a stimulant—a legal one, yes, but a stimulant nonetheless. Perhaps it was the instant camaraderie that came from on drinking coffee out of styrofoam cups and having private conversations in the corner of the student lounge. Whatever it was, it stuck—to this day, if you want to be my friend, and I mean lifelong partner-in-caffeine, you'd better be a coffee drinker instead of a tea drinker. Sorry, chai lovers!

When my best friends and I make plans, it's almost always for coffee. Hundreds of conversations in my life have started with lattes and ended with a promise to not wait so long next time. Friends who go out for a leisurely dinner have to wade through several courses before they get to the good stuff. Over coffee, it usually comes out like this: "I have so much to tell you! First…"

My friends and I will talk for a good hour about family, health, work, and men. Our married friends will remind us single women that life is not always greener on the other side. The divorced friends chime in with dating stories, pledges to never date again, and, yes, even the occasional musings about getting married again. We all celebrate stories of our kids with pictures and videos. We have a world of experience to share. The most dramatic announcements, like starting a new business or moving to a new city, always come after we are down to a quarter cup, and there are refills all around.

Every good friend knows when it's time to let your friends talk without interruption. It will be your time at some point, and that's why we all take turns being a patient (albeit caffeinated), understanding sounding board.

At the end of every coffee date, my friends and I exercise the "Five Minute Rule." This rule states that we are allowed to talk celebrity news for exactly five minutes before we leave. We cover (in this order) Robert Downey Jr., Gwyneth Paltrow, Madonna, Colin Farrell, Joaquin, and J. Lo before devoting the final minute to the latest Real Housewives franchise. Who'd want to spend any more time on celebrity gossip when our lives are much more interesting?

My best friends are coffee drinkers, just like me. Whether we're meeting at Peet's, Starbucks, or the local indie café, or catching up over a Keurig cup at home, my friends get my full, caffeinated attention, and I get theirs. This kind of friendship is too precious to waste on tea, or—heaven forbid—decaf.

My Best Friend, Madonna

Sheila Dolan

Madonna is my spirit animal, my inspiration, and, unbeknownst to her, my best friend. I've always felt very close to Madonna and yet, so, *so* far away. We are exactly the same age, born under complementary sun signs, my Libra to her Leo. Together we resist the ravages of time by often dressing inappropriately, although I am the kind of best friend who will always admit, "Yes, Madonna, that corset looks better on you." In classic Libra form, I'm always the diplomat. Besides, you wouldn't want to ignite Madonna's vain and stubborn lioness. What do you think happened to her "best friend" Sandra Berhardt? That's right, she was banished from Madonna's kingdom over a fight for the spotlight.

If Madonna lived closer to me, I know we'd share more than bad clothes and bad relationship advice. Leos may love to lavish their friends with gifts, but the only real prize I'd want from my Leo best friend is a peek of the wild side. As a Libra, I'm on the eternal search for true love, timeless beauty, and that elusive sense of balance—but underneath it all, I actually crave loud house music, strobe lights, and seedy clubs on the bad side of town. That's why having Madonna's security guards would really come in handy. Plus, my naturally restrained demeanor needs Leo's fiery, adventurous energy.

How would I keep this too-good-to-be-true friendship going? That's easy. The Leo is yours forever if you shower her with praise. Being a people pleaser, I'd start with praising Madonna's crowning glory, her hair. Leos love their manes, and I intend to give her plenty of compliments on her color, cut and style. In return, I expect her to help me decide between leave-in conditioner, mousse, and hairspray. My annoying indecisiveness will be tamed by Madonna's controlling personality. Win-win!

Let's talk about reinventions. Madonna and I share this life philosophy: If something or someone is not working, make a quick, radical change to save face. (It's all about the face. We Leos and Libras share a vanity about our looks, and Madonna is fortunate enough to have a team of ten to help her maintain.) Her marriage to Sean Penn lasted only two years; her best friends (me included) knew that Sean was no good for her. True to her sign, when the marriage first fell apart Madonna indulged in some melodrama, which in my Libra opinion was simply uncouth, but I kept that feeling to myself. In the words of my best pal herself, *Papa don't preach*, and neither do best friends. There's just nothing you can do when your best friend wants to marry Sean Penn. I knew my job was to be there for her and use a tried-and-true Libra tactic: suppress and deny. I'd decided that were we to talk, I'd suggest that she just pretend the marriage never happened—and that's when she rebounded like the head of the lion pride should with an impressive post-Sean dating steak that included Warren Beatty, Antonio Banderas, and Lenny Kravitz. That's my multicultural Leo! That's my Material Girl!

I had my own entanglements after a long marriage, followed by a self-prescribed hiatus and countless years of embarrassing internet dating. If there's one thing Libras and Leos can't endure, it's being embarrassed. Why do you think Madonna's iconic wardrobe malfunction at the Video Music Awards in 1984 (involving a white stiletto and a Bengal tiger) was so brilliantly aborted with one swift dive toward the floor? Madonna might not have approved of my lowering of standards during my "dating" period, but she'd definitely have applauded my rapid rate of turnover. I distinctly remember one Match.com pre-date phone call, when the gentleman caller suggested we meet at a "sandwich shop." A sandwich shop! Who even says that? Given my gentle Libra sensibilities, I was pretty sure I'd be soon be committing dating hari-kiri, so I politely hung up the phone and called it a day. Libras like the thrill of rejection without a lot of fuss.

Through the years of short-term liaisons, I kept two essential lessons from my Leo best friend in the forefront of my mind: Express Yourself and Beauty Is Where You Find It. I made good use of the first lesson when I expressed deep shock on a date said he didn't feel like he had to buy me a cup of coffee, even though he'd invited me out for coffee. An example of the second lesson is when I found beauty in a secluded garden where I waited for one no-show date for more than an hour. And after one uncharacteristically loud breakup scene, I found (or rather, bought) beauty at the Bobbi Brown counter at Nordstrom.

We have actual best friends and we have virtual best friends. They both provide the laughs, support, and inspiration we need to carry on for another day. I'm grateful that the confident, ambitious, and encouraging Madonna has given me decades of inspiration. She taught me that there's noting wrong with wanting to be dripping in diamonds and pearls, but don't expect a man to provide them for you. (So based on my best friend's example, back in 2002 I spent an entire paycheck on my very own minuscule diamond earrings.) From her, I've learned that at the end of the day, the only person you can rely on is yourself, and everyone must stand alone and... jeez, so many lessons... .like... invest in heavily supportive undergarments... and hire the best backup dancers you can... and date backup dancers... and marry a backup dancer... and never, ever let people see your boob, unless it's part of the act.

Thank you, Mad Dog.

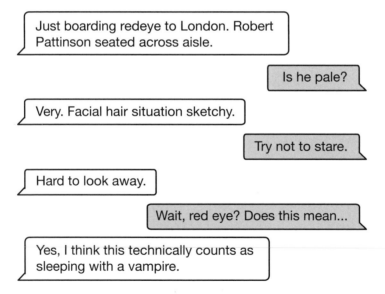

 FICTIONAL FRIENDS

If Madonna is Sheila's best friend, who's your fictional BFF?
We asked, and the Satellite Sisterhood responded:

Molly Ringwald	Tina Fey	Hermione Granger
Murphy Brown	Dorothy Parker	America Ferrera
Lorelai Gilmore	Trisha Yearwood	Judy Blume
Sookie Sackhouse	Maisie Dobbs	Teri Hatcher
Jimmy Fallon	Nancy Drew	Laura Linney
Tituss Burgess	Miss Marple	Liz Dolan
Tim Gunn	Bridget Jones	Anne of Green Gables
Michelle Obama	Lucy Liu	Jennifer Lawrence
Ruth Bader Ginsberg	Shonda Rimes	Jennifer Weiner
Maya Angelou	Molly from Mike and	Jen Lancaster
Lisa Simpson	Molly	Jo March

Laura Ingalls Wilder
Ramona Quimby
Kristen Wiig
Beyoncé
Rachel
Ellen
Oprah
Piglet
Daisy
Lady Rose
Queen Latifah
Sandra Oh
Frida Kahlo

Kay Scarpetta
Mindy Kaling
Amy Poehler
Amy Tan
Jhumpa Lahiri
Katniss Everdeen
Joan Rivers
Julianne Moore
Tig Notaro
Lena Dunham
Meryl Streep
Jennifer Garner
Carrie Bradshaw

Robin Roberts
Kelly Ripa
Anna Quindlen
Rhoda Morgenstern
Ethel Mertz
Phoebe Buffay
Tami Taylor
Gayle King
Taylor Swift
Mary J. Blige
Elizabeth Bennet

WHEN SOMETHING HARD THIS WAY COMES
Ruth Marantz

My life has always been driven by friendships. Apart from a brief shy period, I've always been drawn to other humans. I like listening to conversations and seeing what people carry in their purse. I like to talk and, even more importantly, to be heard. Perhaps my socialbility comes from growing up in downtown Manhattan and always being surrounded by people. When I was little, I was always asking to have a playdate, or a sleepover, or sometimes, if I was feeling lucky, a double sleepover. I remember when I realized how awesome a playdate was. You could actually watch *Dirty Dancing* fifty times in a row. I was fortunate enough to have a good group of girlfriends who had my back, and I liked being engaged all the time.

My friendships were all fine and good—until the dark days of middle school. For some reason, my reputation in said school became an issue that people seemed to feel they needed to take sides on. Cliques replaced friendships; it was everyone for herself or himself. Puberty, rumors, horrific bullying by the boys in my class… the icing on the cake was my parents' divorce. I needed my friends, but instead I internalized my emotions. For the first time in my life, I turned inward. Even at thirteen, I realized the importance of my friends; the idea that these friendships could disintegrate over rumors was terrifying.

Once high school hit, I made a vow to myself that I didn't need to be friends with everyone, just a few good people. I decided to leave that that drama in middle school. I invested my time with the right people, and I'm still friends with them to this day. They are my sisters, my family— much more than just friends.

Then came a very confusing time in my twenties when it seemed like everyone in my circle at a certain point "needed to leave New York" and moved away. Still, I felt fortunate then. I had friends, I was a good friend, and those relationships made me feel good about myself. My life in my early twenties was a haze of roughly twenty-three different jobs, lots of different places to call home, and many bad personal-style decisions. When I turned 25, I noticed there were fewer people who I wanted to call, but still, I was in pretty good shape, friend-wise.

Then came a truly horrific time, which hit in my late twenties and brought an unprecedented amount of hardship. Without getting into all the gory details, I dealt with loss, trauma, and grief on a deep level. I lost my father, my grandparents, my cat—it seemed everyone around me was dying.

And that's when my friends showed up. Some called me in the ICU or sent cookies for my dad's memorial. Some sent stupid texts that made me forget about my grief for just a minute. Some even flew across the country to give me a hug. During this challenging time, I realized something: All that time I'd put into fostering and nurturing friendships, and in being a friend to others, came back to me when I truly needed help surviving. This is the beauty of friendship.

There are times when you need to be lifted off the floor. When you need someone to open your curtains and tell you to get out of bed and stop feeling sorry for yourself. A good friend will bring you pad Thai and tell you things you don't want to hear. You can call a good friend at an ungodly hour or when you're convinced you've left the gas running and your house is on fire. I know, because that's what good friends have done for me.

In my thirties, I value my friendships in a completely different way than I did when I was first on a playdate. I see now how these relationships develop, shift, and change throughout your life. A friendship is not a constant; it's more like a plant in need of water and sunlight. The truth is, our lives can suddenly fall apart, and it can take something overwhelming to happen for us to realize how much we need one another. I was lucky to have good people close to me when I was hit with hard times.

How to Save Money on Birthday Gifts by Discussing Politics on Facebook
Vera Smith

During recent elections and other political events, I noticed many people on Facebook complaining about how they'd had to "unfriend" their friends. Now a proud Texan, I grew up in the former USSR, went to a graduate school in the UK, and traveled throughout Asia, Africa, and Europe as a consultant for international organizations like the World Bank. My Facebook friends are of very diverse backgrounds: conservative, socialist, Muslim, Jewish, atheist, etc. I see political outbursts on a variety of subjects on Facebook all the time, but I never unfriend the posters because of it. Instead, I don't engage by commenting or liking these posts, and if discussions turn particularly heated, I hide them.

A few months ago, however, I was scanning my Facebook page and, along with some cute baby pictures and links to stories like *How to be happy and healthy in your mid-30s,* I saw many posts on the conflict in the Ukraine, including one called *12 Ways in Which Putin's Rhetoric Resembles Germany in the 1930s.* "Indeed," I thought, "the parallels between today's Russia and Nazi Germany are so obvious! How come more people don't see this?" So I "liked" the article. As I kept scrolling down the page, I saw other posts on the topic that called for awarding the Nobel Peace Prize to Putin for rescuing the Crimea from "Ukrainian fascists." "Poor bastards," I thought, rolling my eyes. "Don't they realize that they are victims of the KGB-style propaganda machine?"

The next day I got a Skype call from my best friend, who lives in Moscow. Anna and I have been friends since we were seven back in the former Soviet country of Kyrgyzstan. Our friendship has grown stronger even though we've lived in different countries for the past decade. Anna is an executive at a Russian branch of a large American corporation, and she regularly visits the U.S., even spending a few months on an assignment at the company's West Coast headquarters last year.

We rarely discuss politics, mostly because we have more important things to talk about, like our lives. On this particular Skype call, we covered our children, parents, grandparents, and her plans for the next trip to the U.S. Near the end of the conversation, she reluctantly asked me about the article on Putin and Nazi Germany that I had "liked." "I'm curious," Anna said. "Do you really believe what they report in the American media? I've always noticed how biased the American news is."

I tried to defend my point by saying that it was clear to me that Russia was acting as an aggressor, despite Putin's propaganda trying to prove otherwise.

"Your take on propaganda is… hmm… interesting," Anna said. "Are you sure it's just Putin's propaganda?" She went quiet and then added, "There are many sides to the conflict. I hoped you could see that." I heard anxiety and disappointment in her voice. I decided not to press my point and switched the topic back to our children.

In the following days, I thought more about our conversation. I had angry debates with Anna in my head. How could she not see past the Russian government's TV reports? She's a smart and generally skeptical person. She's spent so much time in the West. Did not she see what was really going on in the Ukraine? I have so much in common with Anna, and yet she and I have ended up holding polar-opposite views on such an important issue. First I was confused, and then hurt, and, finally, I began to doubt my own political convictions.

I spent time reflecting on how my own political views have been shaped, and how I have perceived opinions on the other side of the debate. My deep respect for Anna made me look closer at the position of Putin's supporters. Where are they coming from? Surely not all of them are ignorant, brainwashed, or just plain evil, as is implied by the anti-Russia media.

Some political researchers claim that social media enhances the political process. Perhaps that's true, but I believe there is a flipside: that social media contributes to the polarization of political views. Inflammatory posts and intolerant opinions increasingly drive us to the extremes of the political spectrum, and the room for moderate debate and compromise is shrinking. Only our close friends who have different ideological preferences help keep us informed and in check.

I have not changed my position on the Ukrainian conflict, and I have not stopped using Facebook or other social media. I don't, however, see the picture as quite so black and white anymore. I had to admit that I was looking at the issue from a certain ideological position—and it wasn't neutral. My love for Anna helped to overcome my prejudice and to understand, though not accept, the arguments on the other side of the debate It's not just a matter of "good guys on our side" and "bad guys on their side." In reality, the picture is complex, with many forces on both sides pursuing their own agendas.

While I think it's generally smart to avoid political and ideological discussions with close friends who don't share our views, it's not always an option, particularly now, when a big part of our social and intellectual lives takes place online rather than one-on-one. The role of our friends is to help us pause and think critically about an argument instead of frantically posting "proof" in support of our views. The ability to really listen to our friends, and perhaps even change our views in response to strong points they make—not just stubbornly stick to what we know and unfriend our friends—is an important milestone in personal growth.

So, thank you, my dear friend, for making me a more open-minded and tolerant person. (Although I still think Putin is a tyrant☺.)

Liz's "Lean In" Letter to the Editor
(with apologies to Sheryl Sandberg)

I love you, Sheryl Sandberg. You're doing a bang-up job running Facebook, cowriting that "Women at Work" column in the *New York Times*, publishing *Lean In*, and starting LeanIn.org to further the mission of the book.

I couldn't have done better myself. Hahaha. Or LOL, as they say in your world.

You inspire me, and you also seem like a very nice person. I'm happy for you, Sheryl.

There's just one thing. As you see it, work/life balance is always imagined as a seesaw with WORK on one side and FAMILY on the other.

That's all fine, but when do I get to see my friends? You know: have fun, eat too much, and laugh so hard you split your Spanx. Can I lean in to a little more of *that*?

I'm thinking that maybe life is more of a merry-go-round than a seesaw, and everyone's on it together, including my friends. What do you think, Sheryl? Is the merry-go-round metaphor working for you? I know you said that careers are a jungle gym, not a ladder. I agree on that one.

Your Lean In Circles sound very productive, too, Sheryl. I mean it. I'm sure they're great.

I'm just concerned that your Lean In Circles are... well, a little more additional work than I have in mind. They sound nothing like my book club. In that club, we ditched the books altogether so we didn't have to waste time talking about Haruki Murakami and Hilary Mantel when we had so many better things to catch up on.

Frankly, the only leaning in we did was over the lasagna. I hope you aren't disappointed, Sheryl. It's a really fun group. You should stop by some time. Or Facebook in, though you wouldn't get any of the lasagna that way.

Don't get me wrong about work, Sheryl. I am definitely a Leaner-Inner. I 've worked hard, spoken out, and been in the mix my whole career. I sit at the table.

But there's something else that's really important to me about finding professional satisfaction. Workplaces are great places for women to make lifelong friends. Don't take this personally, Sheryl, but before Facebook, the definition of "friends" was different. You had to have *actually met them*. It was called face-to-face, not Facebook. Human contact was the key ingredient. Workplace friends have been a very important part of my life since the beginning of my career. Work is hard, the business environment is demanding, and we all need a cheering section when the going gets tough. That's why these women are so important.

Here are some of my most important friend groups:

The Rumbledolls: When I worked at NIKE, I was part of a running group that met every morning at 6 a.m., rain or shine, mostly rain, it being Portland and all. We were five women who met at work and somehow managed to figure out that we had *lots* more to talk about than the professional environment allowed us. That's what those mornings were about. We talked so much that we even talked ourselves into running the New York City Marathon together. That's why we had a team name. We all finished the race, so as a team we did something none of us could have done as individuals. This was a while ago, Sheryl, so the Rumbledolls never cooked up a Facebook page to keep connected, but we still spend time together in the real world. Or in real time, as they say in your world.

The Half My Agers: One of the things I really love about my current job is that my female colleagues are half my age. Srsly. Half. They're just getting married, just having babies, and they haven't quite figured out that they don't actually need to work all night and every weekend (which provides cover for a wily veteran like me, who has figured that out). It makes for a really fun environment and keeps me on my toes. You probably relate to this, Sheryl. Isn't everyone at Facebook, like, 12?

Girls Nite Productions: I belong to another girl gang. We're women who met in the sports world across all kinds of job: television producers, athletic-gear marketers, on-air talent, professional athletes, network execs. The nature of the business is that we'd run into each other at events like the US Open, the Final Four, and the Olympics. We are your people, Sheryl, total Lean In types, intense and hardworking, but when we're together, we mainly lean in to order a drink at the bar during our regular nights out. Does that count? I think it does.

Here's the truth about workplace friendships: The bond is intense when you create something together, survive a terrible boss together, make a lot of money for your company together, or lose the whole pot in one disastrous move together. Stuck in cubicles for years, on the road together for weeks, holed up in conferences rooms for weekends—but together all the time.

It's great when one of you becomes the boss, and it really sucks when a dozen of you get laid off. Sometimes the jungle gym becomes a jungle. That's when we really need each other. The true friendships you form when you are engaged professionally last way beyond any current job and longer than most actual companies in, say, Silicon Valley.

Not your company though. I'll bet yours lasts forever. (I'm a big fan :))

So thanks for everything you do and say, Sheryl.

I just wanted to speak up, add my ideas, and lean into the subject a little.

As they say in your world, #YoureTheBest.

Dating Advice From Friends
Sheila Dolan

I've been on a lot of bad dates since I re-entered the world of dating in my late 30s. Through all of the pain and heartache, my friends have always been there with the truth, the lies, and the laughs that get you up and over the next hurdle. Here are actual accounts of what friends have said over the years when I "introduced" them to my dates via the short version, which is all one really has at the beginning:

> **Subject: SWM, early 50s, underwater videographer.** Loves movies, biking, and dogs. Looking for a potential soul mate, someone who enjoys the water and deep conversations.
>
> Friend #1: "When was the last time anyone made a living underwater? That's right... Jacques Cousteau... and he's dead!"
>
> Friend #2: "Deep conversations? He's broke."

Friend #3: "You love the water, Sheila! Give him a try. Maybe you can have him film your amazing butterfly stroke underwater."

Subject: DWM, early 60s, retired. Loves golf, dinners out, and museums. Family oriented, serious, and looking for casual dates that could someday lead to marriage.

Friend #1: "You could not hope for anything better at this point. Dinner? Yes. Museums? Meh!"

Friend #2: "Casual dating? When have you ever been casual about dating? At least the golfing will give you hours of free time."

Friend #3: "Family oriented… hmmm… does that mean he wants a family, has a family, or has many families across the country?"

Subject: SWM, late 40s, sound engineer. Loves hiking, photography, and cooking. Seeking active woman who doesn't mind the fact that I don't own a car. Vegan preferred.

Friend #1: "He hikes to work? He must in wicked good shape."

Friend #2: "Does a man without a car have the right to have a preference over your dietary meal plan?"

Friend #3: "Give him a try. If he walks the twenty miles to meet you, then it's real love."

Subject: SWM, mid-50s, writer. Looking for muse, loves out-of-the-way haunts, old cars, and sushi.

Friend#1: "Are you sure he didn't mean booze instead of muse?"

Friend #2: "He is either ashamed to be in public or ashamed of his car."

Friend #3: "You love sushi! Have you ever been a muse before? What does that entail, exactly?"

Subject: SWM, 45, importer/exporter. Looking for older woman who know who she wants; loves flea markets, Hitchcock, and swing dancing.

Friend #1: "Oh, you know what you want… and it is *not him.*"

Friend #2: "This guy just loves *old*. Keep in mind: You are germaphobe who can't even wear your clothes twice in a row. Flea markets are your idea of hell."

Friend #3: "45 is doable! On the downside, he didn't list his profession, but on the upside, swing dancing is a great workout!"

Subject: DBM, 37, roofer. Looking for an older woman who is not sure what she wants, open to all ages and sizes, loves dining al fresco and art walks, will relocate for the right gal.

Friend #1: "He can take a long art walk down a short pier."

Friend #2: "This guy is the dictionary definition of 'flexible'. But hey, if size doesn't matter, you can do as much al fresco dining as you want!"

Friend#3: "If he has enough money to relocate, he's probably not doing too badly!"

Subject: MWM, 40s, eBay consultant. In an open relationship, looking for a weekend friend, enjoys collecting, live music, and ethnic food.

Friend#1: "Just tell him that you are in a closed relationship. With yourself."

Friend #2: "Friendship is good. Weekends are good. Collecting weekend friends: not good."

Friend #3: "I don't know… a nice bowl of hot pho on the weekend sounds nice!"

RAISE YOUR GLASS
WEDDING TOAST TIPS
Meghan Dolan Saporita

There's nothing better than a *great* toast. You've heard at least one. Remember how it inspired laughs, tears, and all emotions in between? It made you feel like you were actually *there* that time at summer camp with the bride, even if you barely knew those people. We always remember a toast like that—the way it made us feel, the way it paid tribute to the toastee, the general sense of love and sisterhood/brotherhood it brought to the room, and how that sense lingered for the rest of the evening.

My personal history of toasting includes my best friend's wedding, my grandmother's recent significant birthday, and my sister Katherine's wedding—three completely unique ladies worth toasting. Coming up with the toast for my sister's wedding was the hardest one; at first, I had absolutely no idea what to say. Aside from being for my one and only sister, I had to give this toast less than a year after she *killed* her toast at my wedding. Oh yeah, Big Sister felt the pressure. So I spent months writing down tidbits, anecdotes, and ideas. Each time I thought of anything, I put a note in my phone or on a legal pad, and eventually, I knew what would work.

What an honor to be asked to give a maid of honor toast. But what pressure! Yes, a toast should be from the heart, and no, it shouldn't be too long, but you know that already. (Thank you, *Wedding Crashers*.) Here's what I've learned in my short history of toasting:

If you've got it, use it. If you just *happen* to have that email from five years ago when she dished to you about her then-new boyfriend, or if you remember the night when you introduced the two of them and what they did or said, or if you have any other documentation or memories of a good gossip session, **you use it**. My best friend's now-husband is another good friend of mine, and I set them up via email years ago when they were both living in Miami for a short time. In my toast, I could actually say, "Let's start at the very beginning. In fact, I can take you back to that exact moment." Then I read an email that included an exchange between my girlfriend and me in which she wrote, "and he's cute!" Gold.

There's no shame in a good theme. This can be as simple or as complex as you like. Sports. Adventure. Love of others. Kindness. Misfits. If you think about it, any decent theme can be used to tie together both your serious and silly comments. For example, the theme for the toast I made for my grandmother was "good buys." She's famous for her bargain purchases, which include travel-size toiletries, Ziploc bags, tissues, toilet paper, and all the other practical items she finds on sale. She has been delivering "Nanny's good buys" to everyone in our family for as long as I can remember. (Not once in my life have I had to buy Ziploc bags.) For her significant birthday party, I had fun talking about all these seemingly insignificant things she does for everyone—and then I brought it around to how much they actually mean.

Flattery will get you everywhere. What woman, especially a bride on her wedding day, doesn't want to hear about how gorgeous/smart/funny/selfless she is? So go for it. Make her day. If you are the person she chose to give this toast, these praises will come easily.

My toast at Katherine's wedding involved poking some fun at my little sis for her indecisive nature. I went with "kindness" as a theme and worked in "Katherine's Interesting Nature of Deciding," aka KIND. Good, right? Feel free to steal it. But I mixed the fun with feeling. Some people said that the way Katherine looked in her wedding dress rivaled the way the incomparable Pippa Middleton looked in *that* dress. They were right—but it's actually my sister who is incomparable. Despite a lifetime of indecision, she knew how to make the decisions that mattered at her wedding: her groom, of course, and that incredible dress. Needless to say, everyone agreed.

Publicly expressing to my little sister just how much I love and admire her was one of the great honors of my life, and it continues to warm my heart thinking back to that toast. In this era of emojis and emails, you don't often get the chance to tell your sister or your best friend or your grandmother how you feel out loud. So if you get the opportunity, raise your glass, raise your voice, and tell her how she's the best. Cheers!

The Worst Wedding Toast
A Mad Lib

Thank you, *whoever you people are* _____. It's such an honor to
                               Name

speak at the wedding of *my homegirl Joey* _____.
                                    Girl's name

My name is *Lola* _____, and for those
                        Girl's name

of you who don't know me, I'm the maid of honor, or as my

bitches _____ like to call me, the
        Plural noun

Queen of All I See _____. I met _Crazy Joey_ _____,
　　　　　　　Term of endearment　　　　　　　　　　　　　　*Girl's name*

the bride, in _the girls' bathroom in high school_ _____. I'll never forget
　　　　　　　　　　　Location

the first thing she said to me. She took one look at me and said,

"_What the hell is wrong with your face?_ _____." We've been friends ever since.
　　　　　　Exclamation

I can't believe that today is her wedding day! I thought for sure that

incarceration _____ would happen first.
　　　　　Life event

But here we are, celebrating _Joey the Hoey_ _____
　　　　　　　　　　　　　　　　Same girl's name

OMG, I'm so drunk I forgot your name

and _____.

Same boy's name

If you've spent any time with the bride and groom, maybe

doing shots   shoplifting

_____ or _____,

Verb -ing   *Verb -ing*

kleptos

then you know what perfect _____ they are.

Plural noun

happy to be alive

That's why my theme today is _____.

Emotion

Because the bride and groom represent the promise that is

happy to be alive

_____. How do I know that?

Same emotion

Because I have the _____ *subpeona* _____ to prove it!
Communication method

Right after their first _____ *STD* _____,
Activity

the bride told me, "_____ *Piece of crap* _____! He's the one."
Exclamation

It's true _____ *psychosis* _____.
Emotion

Does it get any _____ *needier* _____ than that?
Comparative

I still can't recall your name but . . .

_____, I can assure you that
Same boy's name

you are getting one _____ *foxy* _____ and
Adjective

frisky

_____ woman as your wife.
                    Adjective

If you don't believe me, have her tell you about that time she

well, even I can't say that

_____.
              Past-tense verb

                                        Screw Loose

That's why we call her _____.
                                        Nickname

                        Honey Butt

But you can call her _____.
                            Term of endearment

                                    partyin'

So let's raise a glass to this _____ couple.
                                        Adjective

                parents   _parole officers_

And to their _____ and _____
                    Plural noun   *Plural noun*

for supporting the duo in the future, including their plans to

_____be carnies_____. _____Mojo JoJo_____
            Verb   *Same girl's name*

            One day I'll get it

and _____, be
            Same boy's name
            loyal

_____ to each other.
            Adjective
            only ones you've got in court

You're the _____.
            Comparative adjective

Dogs Rule
Liz Dolan

Sorry, humans. In the Best Friends' Department, sometimes only a dog will do.

They have all of the qualities you want in a true friend.

First, dogs are born enthusiasts. Walks! Squirrels! You! Every day is a vacation day for a dog, so they're always up for excitement. But they're not strongly opinionated about what you do together. Lie on the couch and watch a week's worth of *The Daily Show*? Sure! Drive around and do boring errands? That's just more time to hang a head out the car window! Dogs are never *not* enjoying themselves when they're with you. They even love the way you smell, regardless of when you last showered.

Second, they eat anything you serve. They snarf up all the leftovers so you're not tempted. They come running when they hear you opening that bag of chips. They don't require artisanal *anything.* There are no foodie dogs.

Third, dogs don't judge. They don't question your new hair color or challenge your career choice. With dogs, it's all good, all the time.

Fourth, their schedules are wide open. They're never previously booked or too busy to hang out with you. Conversely, they don't complain about your busy schedule. They greet you with the same enthusiasm whether they saw you an hour ago or a week ago.

Fifth, dogs are good listeners. No backtalk. No interrupting.

Finally, dogs are not complicated. They may be passive, or they may be aggressive, but they're never passive/aggressive.

With a dog, what you see is what you get. There is no subtext to a wagging tail.

How You Describe Your Best Friend
A Word Cloud

We asked the Satellite Sistershood for three words to describe a best friend. These word clouds represent the responses we got.

Family

WHEN YOUR FRIENDS ARE YOUR SISTERS
Sheila Dolan

We didn't have a lot of playdates growing up. The word hadn't even been invented in the 1960s. I can still hear our mother say, "Who needs a friend over when you have each other?" So we grew up learning how to be friends as well as sisters and brothers. As we all grew up and moved away, the concept of having plans with outside friends was an adjustment. We already had a built-in network of grown men and women who all liked the five basic essentials: appetizers, a good homemade meal, laughter, sports, and leftovers.

"What are you doing this weekend? Any plans?" This is a typical end-of-the-week question I get from work friends. *Oh, if only I had some fabulous agenda that involved Santa Barbara, the Hollywood Bowl, or Nobu,* I typically think as I smile and try to come up with a good response. There have been many times, though, when I've felt genuine anticipation as I announced, "Oh, I have plans with my sister(s)…"

When I lived in Santa Monica, I had the pleasure of being Liz's Plus One to parties and openings. Plus One status really is the ultimate friends'-night-out scenario. You get to hobnob with folks you'd never have access to in your real world and practice some serious stargazing. I haven't lived near Liz for years now, and I still miss my position as a Plus One—it's the ultimate win-win weekend friend date.

Now that I live close to Lian, she is often my go-to gal for all sorts of weekend activities. There's always a lunch or dinner at her house, at which I am graciously allowed to eat and run. There are my nephews' birthdays, Super Bowl invitations, barbecues, clothes-swap visits, and an occasional aqua Zumba class, which all rate official "weekend-plan" status. What I love about Lian is that she doesn't care if I show up empty-handed or running on empty. I always leave feeling full, both physically and emotionally.

I'm sure that if Monica lived nearby (something I've been trying to convince her of for years), we'd have major weekend plans. There'd be movies, swimming, and lunches. There'd be a lot of people-watching while enjoying freshly brewed iced tea with lemon wedges. Finally, there'd be mutual complaining, shared daydreaming, and, instead of clothes swapping, income swapping when times get tough.

Julie and I definitely would be best friends (I hope) if we lived near each other. Julie would be the yin to my yang. She'd calm me down when things get nuts, and I'd make her laugh when she felt the same. Sprinkled in the sister-friends weekend-plans mix with her would be makeovers, clothes swaps, and, from time to time, a game of tennis just for us.

Yes, we are all adults now, and we all have our own separate (good) friends. But when your friends are your sisters, you're pretty much always guaranteed an invitation when you most need one. Isn't that what friends are for?

It's Just a Turkey: How to Stay Friends With Your Sisters
Lian Dolan

We started Satellite Sisters to celebrate the concept that women could have very different lives but still share a powerful bond built from humor and respect. Since creating Satellite Sisters, I've spent more time with my sisters than I'd have ever imagined as a child, from the usual laughing and crying to building a business together. When you are a "professional" sister, you get a lot of emails about how we manage to work together, vacation together, deal with family issues together—and still stay friends. It's tempting to just credit it to denial and white wine and leave it at that. But I know there's a lot more to it, so I took a closer look at the last several decades of my relationships with my sisters to see what really made a difference.

Forgive and Forget

Let's be clear, I am neither a psychologist nor an officer of the law, so if you and your sisters have some issues in the past that require therapy or jail time, please seek the correct help for those situations. But for most of us with sisters, the issues that may be keeping our relationships from moving forward are small and decades old. They're the tiny little injustices that you've never gotten over. Here's what I advise: Forgive, Forget, then Move On. Make a conscious effort not to dwell in the past. Chances are that there were mistakes made on both sides—when you were seventeen.

Stay Connected

Modern technology makes staying connected easier than ever, so take advantage of it and be a part of your sister's life, even if she lives 3,000 miles away. Don't let actual distance create an emotional distance. Let's say you're the Big City Gal and she's the Suburban Mom; you can find common ground using today's communication tools. It only takes a minute to comment on her Facebook photos of Junior's science project. Small but frequent connections can sustain a relationship even when you can't see each other as often as you would like.

Be Grownup Sisters, Not the Sisters You Were Growing Up

Ah, the family as time capsule. You walk up the front steps of your childhood home as a confident, grown woman; you walk through the door and become an awkward, headgear-wearing preteen being taunted by your beautiful older sister. Sound familiar? One of the most surprising benefits of working with my four sisters as adults is discovering that they'd learned quite a few skills—and gained in emotional intelligence—since they were, say, fifteen. My sisters are smart, talented accomplished women who have won the admiration of others outside their family. Accept that your sisters have matured, and treat them with the same respect afforded them by their peers.

Laugh as Often as Possible

Life is too short to spend a lot of time discussing politics, religion, and/or other explosive issues with your sisters, particularly if these topics fall under the "divisive differences" category. Maybe this sounds gutless if you and your family routinely debate sensitive issues around the dinner table. But I've found that preserving a sibling relationship means focusing on your similarities or, at the very least, approaching serious topics with a equal doses of humor, respect, and humility. You don't need to win every political argument—and then, when you need support and advice during a difficult life transition, you and your sister will have built a strong foundation.

Speaking of Thanksgiving…

According to the mail we get, a lot of sisterly relationships go down
in flames because of Christmas. Or the Fourth of July. Or Grandma's
birthday. One sister wants to have it at her house, and another digs in her
heels for the privilege to host. Then they don't speak for ten years. Find a
compromise or let it go. So what if you never host Thanksgiving? There
are 364 other days of the year to get the family together. An expert on our
radio show gave great advice when I whined about my mother's need to
cook the turkey, even at my house. She said, "It's just a turkey. If it makes
her happy, let her cook the turkey." Right, it's just a turkey.

Six Friends Every Mom Needs
Lian Dolan

The In Case of Emergency Friend

Solid, reliable, carries her cell phone at all times, the ICE friend can literally save your life. Whether it's a medical meltdown or a babysitter bailout, she is there for you and your kids. If you put her down as your emergency contact, you'll have nothing to worry about.

The LOL Friend

Every mother needs one friend who is just a hoot, regaling you with the hilarious story of the evil stomach bug or a school project disaster. Sometimes, motherhood is just not that funny. But an LOL Friend makes you see that it can be—if you lighten up a little bit.

The Ear to the Ground Friend

There's always one woman, usually the mom of an active girl, who knows everything going on at school. Not the gossip, the good stuff. From homework to weekend parties, the Ear to the Ground Friend is an essential go-to resource. For those of us who live at the edges of information (and by that I mean Mothers of Boys), any source for what's happening is always welcome.

The Life Coach Friend

Technically, she's not trained in anything psychological or medical, but the Life Coach Friend really knows how to diagnose you—and then motivate you. One forty-five minute walk with Life Coach Friend and you're updating your resume, signing up for golf lessons, and making a mammogram appointment.

The Frenemy

Sports stars say they need a rival to keep them on their toes, and so do mothers. Chances are, your Frenemy is always one step ahead of you. Her house is cleaner, her kids are smarter, and, her skin has more collagen. But that's okay, because your Frenemy forces you focus on what's really important in your life. Maybe you've lost the skin-elasticity battle, but you're winning the hair-highlighting game.

The No Kids, No Thanks Friend

Every mom needs time away from her life as a mother. Enter the No Kids, No Thanks Friend. She goes to movies! She knows the trendiest restaurants! She still wears pants with non-expandable waistbands! One afternoon with No Kids Friend revives the spirit and reminds you that's there's life outside the laundry room.

FLOATING INTO FRIENDSHIP
Lauren Hinkson

She crossed into our lane. To the end, I will testify that she crossed into our lane. You see, in the New York City public pools there are no lane markers. Only unofficial recognition of what may or may not be a straight line that you imagine between where you are swimming and where someone else is swimming. It is a gentlemen's agreement on boundaries, a rarity in this crowded, hot, and often-smelly August city.

The problem is, the other swimmer claimed that we had crossed into her lane. And she took it to the authorities—the underpaid, sunburned, i-don't-care-if-you-drown-don't-you-dare-ask-me-to-skim-that-hairball-from-the-pool lifeguards. What this rather unpleasant woman (I would testify that she was inexplicably looking for an axe to grind) didn't realize was that she was taking on two young women who were both eight months pregnant. So when we saddled up to the side of the pool at the beckoning of the lifeguards, our ill-fitting maternity Speedos said it all.

This lady was gonna lose the fight.

The thing about New York is that there are thousand chances every day to make friends (or enemies) in small moments. There are just so many people. And it happens. It happens and then it is over: A stranger makes a choice to be your friend for a minute or two, and then they are gone like that train you missed this morning on your way to work.

This experience is even more obvious when you are pregnant or toting around your brand-new baby in your very tired arms:

The bus driver will count out an extra beat to let your swollen body catch up and hop on the cross-town even though you shouldn't be running after a bus when you are ten months pregnant—*it is a moment of friendship*.

An older woman will give you a wink while you sit on the floor-sample ottoman in an uptown department store to nurse your baby, just that little bit of encouragement for your quiet defiance of the truly ugly $10,000 ottoman—*it is a moment of friendship*.

A rowdy teen, who a moment ago was yelling words that made you wish you had noise-canceling headphones for your baby, will go silent as you step off the subway together, and then will lean down to help you carry your hulking stroller up the stairs to the street—*it is a moment of friendship.*

But despite all these beautiful small acts of friendship, I still felt alone after my daughter was born. Eight million potential friends (okay let's be real, maybe two million of those people are friendship material) surrounded me. Eight million bodies bumping into one another, and I was lonely in my Brooklyn apartment with this fresh life teaching me how to be in the world as a mother.

I joined the mommy groups that are divided by three-month intervals of your child's birth date (there are that many new mothers in Brooklyn). I joined the baby and me yoga classes where you do more nursing, rocking, and dead-eyed staring than yoga. I even sat quietly at the playground when school let out with my newborn fast asleep in her stroller just to be near other mothers. The nannies knew what I was up to and welcomed me into their conversations.

Here's the thing though: I wasn't looking for mommy friends. I had the people to complain about sleep training with and the people to find inner peace with and the people to help catch my future toddler as she dangled from the slide. But what I wanted, what I so desperately yearned for, was someone to share in the awe.

I found that person in the pool that day: my swimming buddy who helped me defend our lane. She became the friend who walked laps around our office building with me, arms linked on those hard-to-stand-up days of late pregnancy, talking about the beauty in the world that we'd share with our children, the kindness we'd try to teach them, and the many ways we anticipated we'd fail at our vision of motherhood. This new friend, she understood. She shared in comprehending the magnitude of this transition in our lives.

Our babies arrived just days apart. We are mothers now and we are changed. What I've learned in these first few months with my daughter and from this blossoming friendship is that the people I'll rely on in this new life of motherhood won't necessarily be moms. But they will have to be kind of friends who'll always be ready to throw down at the public pool when someone crosses into your lane.

THE CONDOLENCE CLUB
Lian Dolan

When I think back on that time in my life, I call it the Root Canal Years. I was deep in the mire of what social scientists call the Sandwich Generation, but that name is far too benign for the constant barrage of stress, craziness, guilt, grief, and feeling just plain awful, physically and mentally. No kind of sandwich I know represents feeling that out control of your own life. In short, my aging parents were in decline, my teen boys were engulfed in the teen years, from sports to heartbreak to freak infections to college admissions, and my own career was just that: my own career. As a writer, if I didn't work, I didn't get paid, and with most of my days (and nights) filled with worry, it was hard to lighten up and write funny fiction. I can sum up the years 2011 through 2013 this way: I had five root canals in three years because, as my gentle dentist told me, "You are grinding your teeth to death."

I think that gives you an accurate picture of the stress level.

I found that as my parents' health deteriorated, my social circle got smaller. My father was in the end stages of Alzheimer's when my mother was diagnosed with stage-four cancer. Pretty much everything else with them—eldercare, assisted-living housing, medical appointments—was going poorly. As one of the siblings who lived closest to my parents, I was spending at least several hours a day actively engaged in their care. Some weeks, I'd spend days at a time at their house in Santa Monica, leaving my husband and kids to fend for themselves. When an innocent acquaintance would toss out a casual, "How's it going?" and I answered truthfully, they'd back away in stunned silence. I don't blame them. It was a lot to take in. I only had the energy to explain the harsh realities of the situation to a small circle of friends, people with whom I had history and who knew my parents. I needed to surround myself with friends who would never utter the words, "You know what you should do?" and then suggest that my father do more crosswords or my mother try zinc. We were way past crosswords and zinc.

While I struggled to keep it all together on the home front, in various hospitals and rehab centers, and driving in the never-ending L.A. traffic that added hours onto my caregiving duties, my friends showed up time and time again. I came to think of them as the Condolence Club, a self-appointed circle of people who knew the situation and responded with kindness. Leaving thoughtful messages on the phone or by text, always ending with "No need to call back. Just wanted you to know I'm thinking of you." Meals arrived on my doorstep from a small number of women who knew what I was going through, having just lost a parent themselves, or those who figured I probably hadn't made it to the grocery store that week. There were days when I could barely articulate, "Can you pick up my son here and drop him off there?" but somehow that happened. When you let people help you, they do it, without any need of thanks.

When my mother died just after Thanksgiving 2012, the steady flow of cards and flowers began. Of course, when someone dies, you should send flowers and cards, but when it's your mother who dies, you remember every arrangement, every note. I was so surprised and touched that so many would reach out. Who knew a simple card could be so helpful? Other sent rose bushes because my mother loved roses. (They're in bloom now and look lovely.) Never in my life had I considered acting upon the "in lieu of flowers" line in a person's obituary, but friends searched out my mother's notice in our hometown newspaper and made donations to her charity. I was stunned. More meals came, and though I don't remember what we ate, I remember that they arrived. And that they made a difference. Friends made the effort to come to my mother's funeral, some of whom I hadn't seen in decades, and that was astonishing to me.

When my father died a short ten weeks later, I was almost embarrassed to tell my friends. Their generosity of spirit had been so genuine with my mother's death; I didn't want them to feel obligated to repeat their efforts for my father. But the cards, the flowers, the meals, and the donations came again.

Here's what I know now about being a card-carrying member of the Condolence Club: Every gesture matters. At the darkest moments of your life, a little soup brings light. A card cheers you up. An encouraging text can keep you going. I know, too, that you don't have to wait until someone dies to say, "I'm so sorry." A condolence is an expression of sympathy to someone experiencing sorrow. When I look around these days, I see more sorrow than I did ten years ago, when I was stretched by work and raising young kids. I was focused on my family first, and I admit I missed a lot of opportunities to reach out.

Now I have time to poke my head up and take in more. I see that lots of people need a little sympathy. I'm so sorry about the results. I'm so sorry about the divorce. I'm so sorry that your son is having trouble. I'm so sorry the job didn't work out. I'm so sorry you're feeling down.

There's never a good reason to wait to express kindness.

Play

Happy Birthday to you

A Satellite Sisters Guide to Birthday Parties

21st Birthday Party

What to Expect: A joyous and raucous evening of dancing, drinking, and cabbing it home

Where to Hold It: Dorm room spruced up with little white lights, then move to a dive bar

What to Wear: Wear a bikini if you want. You're 21!

What to Serve: Keep it classy with Trader Joe's "champagne" before the evening gets out of hand

Gifts You'll Get: Nothing, because your friends are all so totally broke

30TH BIRTHDAY PARTY

What to Expect: Genuine excitement that adulthood has finally arrived combined with genuine terror that adulthood has finally arrived

Where to Hold It: That new place that just opened with the good lighting and the cute waiters—you know, the one where you might run into that guy from the gym

What to Wear: LBDs all around

What to Serve: Retro cosmos, because you're feeling very Carrie Bradshaw

Gifts You'll Get: Decent leather goods, because you just scored that promotion

40TH BIRTHDAY PARTY

What to Expect: A sense of accomplishment that you've made it through the prime childbearing years for better or worse—and the absolute need to blow off steam

Where to Hold It: Girls weekend! Preferably a tropical setting, because the humidity makes your skin appear dewy

What to Wear: Sarongs, day and night

What to Serve: Drinks with fruit kabobs, which count as food, drink, *and* detox

Gifts You'll Get: Naughty things, because you're still young

50TH BIRTHDAY PARTY

What to Expect: Emotions all over the map, because, let's face it, the birthday girl is no spring chicken

Where to Hold It: Wine country or wine bar

What to Wear: Light layers

What to Serve: The best wine you can afford

Gifts You'll Get: Scarves to shroud neck

60th Birthday

What to Expect: Good times! You're the youngest in a whole new age group!

Where to Hold It: At somebody's second home in the mountains

What to Wear: European comfort shoes, because you just don't care anymore, in a good way

What to Serve: Decaf coffee

Gifts You'll Get: Books you truly love, ones that will stand the test of time

 ## Funseekers vs. Funsuckers

Funsuckers drag you through the preparatory stages.
Funseekers arrive ready.

Funsuckers always bring the wrong clothes.
Funseekers are content to wear plastic ponchos.

Funsuckers never have an opinion until it's too late.
Funseekers take charge or take direction.

Funsuckers post the spoilers.
Funseekers recommend the next best binge watch.

Funsuckers never put their phones down.
Funseekers put it on vibrate.

Funsuckers think the request for "adults only" applies to other's people's children.
Funseekers think the request for "adults only" is a great excuse to get a babysitter.

Funsuckers fight in public.
Funseekers save it for the ride home.

Funsuckers start with an excuse.
Funseekers start with a grande latte.

Funsuckers itemize the dinner check.
Funseekers throw in an extra twenty.

Funsuckers worry about the parking.
Funseekers offer to drive.

Funsuckers use Facebook as a political platform.
Funseekers post videos of their dog.

Funsuckers edit your e-mails and send them back.
Funseekers congratulate you on a great idea.

Funsuckers constantly reschedule meetings.
Funseekers just want to get the thing over with.

Funsuckers give you the gruesome details of their GI series.
Funseekers recognize the comedic value of the phrase "barium enema."

Funsuckers won't dance.
Funseekers are the first on the floor.

Funsuckers arrive late.
Funseekers stay late.

Funsuckers rule the comments section.
Funseekers hit the like button.

Funsuckers count calories.
Funseekers count cannolis.

Packing List for the Girls' Weekend
Julie Dolan

Twenty years ago, my friend Sarah sent out an email to her college buddies to get together for a women's weekend. Newly single with two young children, she wanted time with her friends. A smallish group showed up for support, and we've been meeting ever since. I couldn't make that first meeting and missed a few others while living abroad, but my friends have always saved me a place.

In the early years, we couldn't afford to fly or take time off from work, so we'd gather at someone's house or in a cheap B&B on the East Coast, where most of the group lived. It wasn't always easy to show up—we had to move heaven, earth, husbands, birds, dogs, and children to make it work. Since that first weekend, Sarah, Carol, Betsy, Lisa, Jan, Leslie, Linda, and I have met every year, usually in the fall and, sometimes again in the spring. Our time together is precious, and over the years we've learned what is really important to bring to a women's weekend. Here's our list.

A name. You've got to give your group a name. We're the Aging Models. One day, early on, we were all lounging outside in the spring sunshine, relishing the brief respite from our jobs, young children, and (in a few cases) problematic husbands. A fellow hotel guest asked if we were all there for a class reunion. Lisa replied, "We're here for a convention of aging models."

Party favors. One time, Jan arrived from Paris with Eiffel Tower earrings for all. Sarah has supplied romance novels. And on a fall trip to Massachusetts, Lisa delivered Wal-Mart orange hunting vests, glitter, and glue. We decorated our vests and had a more confident tromp in the woods during hunting season.

A culture infusion. You need to show up with a recommendation list of books, movies, and TV shows. I've had some lean years where, between work and family, my list was short and weak, but Lisa and Leslie's reading habits always stayed admirable. While I've never read all the recommended books, I feel smarter just having the list pinned to my bulletin board.

Sleepwear. No sexy nighties needed. Locate your ancient Lanz nightgown and get flanneled. Carol leads the subgroup that rises early to drink coffee and talk. Socks, slippers, and bathrobes are essential gear.

Don't bother with makeup. Unless it's some new product that's going to make us all look younger. The year mineral makeup burst on to the scene, Linda led a mineral makeup tutorial. By the following year, we'd all abandoned the miracle minerals, but for at least one weekend, we glowed.

Food. Lunch and dinner reservations with seven highly opinionated women can be problematic. I think our picture is still on the kitchen wall of a Portland, Maine restaurant that served us questionable hanger steaks one year. Believe me, that waiter won't try the explanation he gave the Aging Models again. ("The chef says the hanger steak is located next to the kidney and that's why it tastes funny.") We eat in, not out—because it's more fun, and Linda makes a better meal anyway.

Wine. Oh sure, there's some of this, but, honestly, a lot less than you'd think. The last couple of years, it's been more seltzer, less sauvignon blanc.

Your issues and your opinions. Want to quit your job? Problem with a teenage son? Wondering how to plan an out-of-town rehearsal dinner?

No worries. We'll talk you off that ledge, shore up your confidence, or send a detailed floor plan on Monday. Our group comes to the weekend with plenty of advice and experience, plus the confidence to tell you exactly what you need to do with your life.

Rituals. We've worked out the perfect program, so we're sticking to it. Pre-weekend, texts and emails fly regarding modes of transportation, arrival and departure times, menu options, supplies, and planned activities. We always cook the Friday-night dinner and plan a big breakfast for Sunday morning. Saturday is walk/hike/activity time.

No spa appointments. Individual treatments take away from group conversation. Walks, runs, apple picking, museums, group exercise, garden tours, and county fairs will work. We prefer activities that promote group harmony and fun. Shopping is okay, but only if you all buy the same thing, like the woven napkins we all bought once in Petersham, MA. And remember, if you try on clothes, we're going to tell you how you really look in them.

Occasional guests. We've had great times with special guests who attended one of our weekends, but you should proceed cautiously, as a guest may tip the harmonic balance of the group. As for spouses and partners, we've come dangerously close to planning a weekend with them but then stepped back from that edge. We've been meeting for only twenty years, and maybe it's just too soon to bring our other halves.

Memories. We lost Betsy to cancer two years ago. There was a strong showing of Aging Models at her funeral, and she's left a big hole in our group. Since then, weekends away always include some reflection about the conversations and adventures we shared with her. Now that we've reach the twenty-year mark, Sarah is working on a photo album to chronicle our friendships. And we're all trying to remember if we went to Cape May in the spring of 1999 or '98.

 Go Outside and Play
Julie Dolan

My husband and I moved to Moscow in 2002, thanks to his work. When people ask what it was like to live in Russia for nearly five years, I always say that it was intensely wonderful and intensely not wonderful. But having moved around a bit, I've learned that you'd better try to love where you live. In Russia, trying to love where you live required extra effort, but it finally resulted in some spectacular experiences.

Russian winters start in October and hanging on well into April. That first December, I felt sure that I wasn't meant for a Moscow winter. I just wanted to stay in my apartment, sip tea or something stronger, and reread *Anna Karenina*. However, it soon became clear to both me and my husband that if I stayed inside all day by myself, I would either go mad or be very mad at him. I decided it was best to follow the order our mother issued every single afternoon when we were growing up: "Go outside and play." So I joined the cross-country skiing group associated with the International Women's Club of Moscow.

And that's how I learned that one of the ironies of living in Moscow is that the only way to survive the brutal winters is to go outside, even when the thermometer reads minus fifteen. What I liked about that cross-country-ski organization is that there were no bylaws to approve or attendance to take—you just showed up with your skis. If you didn't have skis or didn't know how to put them on, someone was always willing to lend a pair or advice. This was a "no experience necessary" group of expat women from Germany, Britain, Canada, and, of course, the Nordic countries. It was very easygoing, but I admit that when I detected a Scandinavian accent, or if someone mentioned that she used to ski to school as a girl, I'd let her go ahead of me in the line. *Please, ski on, Birgit!*

I wore long underwear, two pairs of socks, gloves and glove liners, a scarf and hat, insulated pants, and multiple layers on top that could be zipped up or off depending how much steam we'd generate skiing the tracks. You didn't need a chic ski outfit or makeup. In fact, sometimes I'd run into a few of my skiing friends at indoor events for which we'd spent a little more time on grooming, and we wouldn't recognize one another at first.

A key ingredient in our group was our leader, Lisa, a kind, patient woman who sent out excellent directions. Each Thursday, as few as six or as many as twenty women showed up at the designated spot, as per Lisa's map. We skied in parks, forests, and on the frozen Moscow River. It seemed that everyone in Moscow had been given the same motherly advice to go outside and play. We passed flocks of schoolchildren in PE classes, pairs of pensioners, single men in racing suits skate-skiing at high speeds, and bunches of young mothers teaching their toddlers to sled and ski, the children bundled in so many layers that they resembled Ewoks. Ice fisherman, packs of stray dogs, birds trying to stay warm—we skied past all of them in the forests of Moscow.

And while we skied, we talked, although were challenged by being strung out in a single line on a cross-country ski trail. Our conversations were like the childhood game of telephone. One Thursday, a woman at the back of the line was telling us what she'd observed at a banya as a Russian woman prepped for a big Valentine's Day. Those of us at the front of the line kept having to ask the storyteller at the back of the line to shout out key details, and they'd get passed up the line. The specifics of the Russian woman snipping and pruning her own Valentine down there was too good to be true, and it got wilder and funnier as it came up the ski line.

The skiing, the talking, and the camaraderie were all over in a couple of hours, and that was good, too.

While I'm happy that my Russian visa has expired and I now live closer to family and friends, I miss my cross-country ski girls. We had good, cold fun. I'm sure that's why I love my Texas tennis team. Friends playing together—you can't beat that.

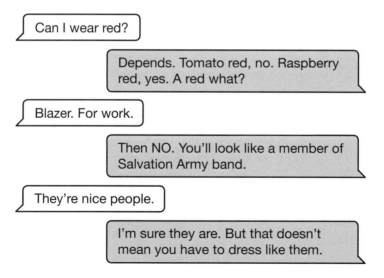

> Can I wear red?

> Depends. Tomato red, no. Raspberry red, yes. A red what?

> Blazer. For work.

> Then NO. You'll look like a member of Salvation Army band.

> They're nice people.

> I'm sure they are. But that doesn't mean you have to dress like them.

What's Your Satellite Sister Group Called?

We asked, and the Satellite Sisterhood delivered. Yes, it turns out that you do have a special name for your group of girlfriends. The origin stories are as fun as the names. There are Girls, Gals, Sisters, Divas, Goddesses, Ladies, Queens, Chicas, Moms, and plenty of Babes. A special shout-out to that posse of dental hygienists who call themselves the Hot Hygiene Babes.

55 Alive!

The Cosmo Girls

The Pretty Nice Mean Girls

The Academy Girls

The Valley Girls

The Pickles

The Fun Buns

The Knit Wits

The Crowbars

Club Murray

Partners in Crime

Girls Night Out

The Badunkadunk Busters

The Pink Ladies

The Pretty Ladies
Bookin' Babes
Beautiful Babes
Bitchin' Babes
Birthday Babes
Beach Babes
Reunion Babes
Water Babes
Hot Hygiene Babes
Dinner Divas
GCHS Cougars
The Walkie Talkies
Otie's Angels
Happy School
The HDKs
The Stalls
The Krazy Kappas
The Grinds
The Irlandistas
The Book Goddesses
The Circle

The Posse
The Yayas
The Petite Yayas
The Red Hots
The Bookettes
The golf4girls
The Quad Gs
The Renegade Six
The Core 8
The Great8
The Fab Four
The Female Fantasies
The Strand Cruisers
The Mighty Chicas
The Queens of the Court
The Weanies
The Thunder Eggs
The Gal Pals
The PTA Moms
The Baking Party
The Garden Club

The Executive Committee
The Spokes-Women Motorcycle Club
The Library Goddesses
The Poker Gals

The Bowheads
Sisterhood of the Shrimp
Sistas of the Hollow
Sisters of the Cloth
Sisterhood of the Traveling Aunts

Change

WHAT MY FRIENDS HAVE TAUGHT ME AT 15
Fiona Dolan

You may not be into the same things as your friends, but that shouldn't change your friendship

It's okay to decline an invitation

Pick your friends over boys, never the other way around

Wear what you feel confident in

Putting on a cute outfit will make you feel better

Go out and get some fresh air, even if you don't feel like it

Some people just aren't going to like you, even if you've never talked to them before

Often times you only get one chance, so make it count

Don't push someone to do something they aren't ready for

Don't push yourself to do something you aren't ready for

Know your boundaries

Go out for the team, even if you're afraid you'll get cut

Stop spending so much money on food

Drink green tea

Eat a home-cooked meal

Sometimes you're going to cry and no one is going to care

Quite often yours will be the shoulder someone is crying on,
    so get used to it

Maturing is a good thing

Don't leave your headphones at home

Don't be afraid to tell the truth

Don't be afraid to be confident

Stop lying to your parents

Remember they were teenagers once

Just because your dad went to Woodstock doesn't mean he's going
    to let you go to Coachella

Focus on your grades

Stop procrastinating on your homework

Don't be jealous of your brother if he's better than you at some things

Take more risks

How many likes you get on a photo doesn't matter

Stop being so negative

Form your own opinions

Don't be too trusting of people

Even "nice" guys will use you

Stick with your instincts

Follow through with your promises

Don't let the good ones go

Stop over thinking

Let yourself be happy

Blasting Taylor Swift in the car is always a good idea

WHAT MY FRIENDS HAVE TAUGHT ME IN MY 20S
Katherine Dolan

Graduating from college doesn't mean you have it all figured out

Turning 25 is more exciting than turning 21

A good pair of boots is worth the money

A "hot stone nurturing and rejuvenating pedicure with antioxidants" at the nail salon is not

Sleep actually matters

Manners actually matter

Start your 401K

Don't show up to a party empty-handed

A good friend and a good roommate can be mutually exclusive

A 400-square-foot NYC apartment is gigantic when you're 22

A 400-square-foot NYC apartment is unlivable when you're 27

Not too many good things happen after 2 a.m., but you need to experience them to realize that

Your first job will lead to some great friends, good experience, and tears—lots of tears

Learning to say no is a necessary skill for your sanity

Self-respect is a necessary skill for your happiness

Basic cooking skills are a must

No one can survive without pasta or toast

There is nothing quite like a home-cooked meal

Texting is not appropriate for all conversations

Music cures most things

Studying abroad is a unique type of freedom

You won't love all of your girlfriends' significant others, but it's not about you

Getting engaged is about so much more than the ring

Marriage doesn't make you boring, only being boring does that

Your friends having children is a crazy and wonderful thing

You don't need a new dress for every friend's wedding

Never trust a man's age or height on Tinder

Road trips are the best

A phone call home to check in makes a big difference

Your siblings are different people than they were as angsty teenagers

Your parents are real people with real emotions

You are turning into your parents

Remember that 400-square-foot NYC apartment? You should've bought it when the market was bad

I'm SO sorry for going all bridezilla on you. Drinks on me? #ytb

What My Friends Have Taught Me in My 30s

A decent haircut is worth the money

So is a decent couch

It's okay to covet another women's handbag, but not her fiancée

The number of bridesmaids should drop dramatically after a bride reaches 30

There's no perfect time to have a baby

There's no perfect childcare situation

Nothing prepares you for motherhood

Nothing prepares your marriage for parenthood

A dog is not a child

Nine months to gain the weight, nine years to lose it

You may want to wear sweats all day, but don't

Black boots pull any outfit together

Sunscreen, sunscreen, sunscreen

Defend the décolletage

Gardening replaces clubbing as weekend activity

Some people work for a living

Some people work really, really hard for a living

Some people have these things called trust funds

Your babysitter may make more than you

That new guy in your office may make more than you

Being the boss is very different than being the rising star

Being the school auction chair will kill you

When it comes to volunteer work, no good deed goes unpunished

Family vacations are a lot of work

You'll never win the holiday-card competition

Singles have a second home; marrieds have a second mortgage

It's not too late to go to grad school

It may be too late to go to Coachella

If you've still got it, flaunt it

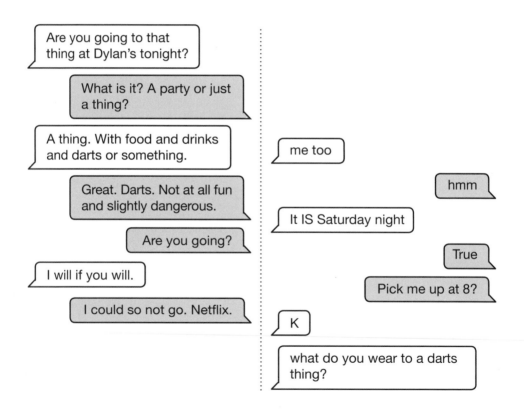

What My Friends Have Taught Me in My 40s

The Power Decade is exhausting

40 is sexier than 49

No diet stops metabolic slowdown

Tailored is more slimming than flowing

Charcoal gray makes you look younger than black

Nobody takes sides in the Mommy Wars anymore because the stay-at-home moms went back to work and the working moms are burned out

Aging parents + cranky teenagers = hair loss

Occasionally Democrats vote Republican

Occasionally Republicans vote Democratic

Recovery from bunion surgery is more painful than recovery
    from childbirth

You can wax almost any part of your body, but that doesn't mean
    you should

Perimenopause lasts decades

Hormones come in pellets

Buy each other birthday gifts, because nobody else cares

Divorce is not the slightest bit funny

Marriage better be funny or you're in trouble

Moisturize, moisturize, moisturize

You never regret not having that third glass of wine

If you miss the tech bandwagon, you'll never get back on board

Nothing beats driving around with the seat heater on

When your eyes start to go, not only can't you read the paper,
    you can't see to pluck your eyebrows

It's now or never when it comes to making it big in your career

Nobody's child is perfect

Nobody's marriage is perfect

Nobody's body is perfect

Everybody's got something; everybody has bad years

Keeping score doesn't matter anymore

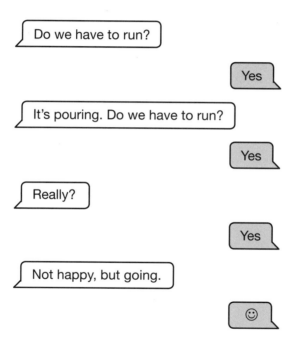

What My Friends Have Taught Me in My 50s

Big necklaces rule

Damn cancer

Don't stop now. Press on. Fight with every bone in your body

If you blow this decade, you're in real trouble for the final third of your life

Don't reference the JFK assassination around young co-workers

Knock off a few major foods groups every year

Start with salt

Your kids will end up at the right college or not, and it will be okay

The college drop-off is hard, but you'll get over it

The empty nest is pretty sweet

You never stop being a parent

Memorize, internalize, and repeat often

Preserve, protect, and defend

Lift, layer, and compress

Yes, you do have to have a colonoscopy

The prep is worse than the procedure

There is nothing good about menopause—nothing

Tint your brows and lashes

You cannot control or manage aging parents. Pray for patience

Your son's text messaging app is not disabled, he's just not responding

There's no filter anymore

It's not your imagination—you are invisible

Post-It notes from now on

Smile when you can't remember

Gloves help

We all prayed to a false idol: Sharon Stone

Love the ones you're with; it's the best youth tonic there is

Zip it

WHAT MY FRIENDS HAVE TAUGHT ME AT 60
Julie Dolan

Turning 60 is better than turning 50

You're the youngest in a whole new category

Being a grandparent is even better than the hype

It's all about family and friends

You can't make new old friends

I'm never going to stop missing my late parents

I'll always want to call my mother every day

Keep moving

Prayer is time well spent

Everyone has regrets

There's a tremendous satisfaction in making it this far

You need less stuff

Use your fine china for weekday suppers

Glucosamine, Retin-A, and a ceramide moisturizer

A long marriage is an amazing thing

The correct response to adult children for *any* situation is, "I know
you'll make the right decision"

It's very, very sweet when your children find their mates

Consider your daughters-in-law your daughters

Up next: Machu Picchu, Taj Mahal, and tea with the Queen

Don't skip your annual physicals

Do skip the black and gray

Wear white and cream

You have to forgive

Save your shoulders: use smaller purses

Don't forget: call your satellite sisters

 RUTBUSTERS

We were in a rut, and you came along and busted us out. Thank you, Rutbuster friends! You're the best.

RUT	**BUSTER**
Tomato Soup	Pho
Tuna Salad	Kale Salad
Lean Cuisine	Kale Salad
Caesar Salad	Kale Salad
Diet Coke	Herbal Iced Tea
Spa Vacation	Road Trip
Honeybaked Ham	Mashed Potato Bar
Power Walking	Soul Cycle
Decorator's White	Raw Umber
Foils	Balayage

Co-dependency	Rehab
Down Vests	Capes
Chevron Stripes	Flame Stitch
French Tips	Nail Art
Bitch Sessions	Ted Talks
Carole King	Norah Jones
Norah Jones	Adele
Adele	Original Cast Recording of the Carole King musical
Good Will Hunting	*I Bought a Zoo*
Ben Affleck	Benedict Cumberbatch
Watching TV on Couch	Watching Netflix on Couch

Bad Advice from Good Friends

We love you, but you said it, and you can't deny it. We don't hold it against you too much. But just so you don't repeat it to anyone else you care about, here's our list of Bad Advice from Good Friends.

Don't miss Graceland!
Wear a snappy hat to the interview.
Everybody parks here.
Order the oysters.
Just tell him the way you really feel.
Take astronomy. It's easy.
All this house needs is a little TLC.
You don't have to declare that as income.
Yes, absolutely put your picture on your resume.
You don't need a passport to go there.

Kilts are back in.

You'd look hot as a redhead.

It's totally safe to get Botox at a nail salon.

Go to my colonics girl. She's a genius.

You work hard. Your boss will see that. You don't need to ask for a raise.

Your mother-in-law won't care if you miss one Christmas.

Yes, have a third. You'll barely notice the new baby.

You have to get a puppy.

Banks forgive student loans.

Beef Wellington is really easy to make.

Flambé it.

It just says Double Black, but you can handle it.

You'll love the State Fair.

RVing is the way to go.

We can split the condo nine ways. It'll be fun.

Let's make it a couples' shower. Men love to be included.

Antibiotics will take care of that.

You don't need to stretch beforehand.

That suit is flattering on everyone.

Marry him. He'll change.

 # FINDING MY TRIBE
Lian Dolan

I'm on a quest for a tribe. It seems my days are numbered on a few of my current social circles. As my children matriculate from high school and age out of youth sports, I find myself in need of a sense of belonging. I'm on the hunt for a ready-made pack of friends and acquaintances based on some shared interest, mascot, or zip code.

This is familiar territory. When I first moved to Pasadena, Land of Many Ancient Tribes and Country Club Alliances, I was a Girl Without People. A young bride, arriving on the wings of love to move in with my new husband, I'd lived many places and had adjusted to lots of new environments, but nothing prepared me for breaking into the guarded Pasadena inner circle. My husband didn't appear to have retained his best friend from fourth grade or a deep connection to a former school, the way every other person in town had. He was an independent, and that meant I was friendless. I worked freelance out of our spare bedroom, so I had no coworkers, and my two college pals who lived in my new area code relocated to the other side of the country shortly after my arrival. (Something I said?) I was desperate to interact with somebody, *anybody* besides the mailman and the ice cream truck guy.

Clearly some tribes in town simply weren't going to be available to me, like the My House Is Giant and Architecturally Significant crowd or the select few who occupied the lofty My Family's Been Here for Four Generations tier. I accepted that I was out of their leagues and rightly so, with my Oregon plates and unpolished nails. Ditto the powerful volunteer organizations that required large amounts of time or money, preferably both. (I didn't really have either.) Groups of people gathered in the celebration of Bruins or Bears or Trojans or Cardinals, but I was a Sagehen, and no one gathered in their name. Squads of runners and cyclists circled the Rose Bowl, but I couldn't quite get in on the action, shunning any activity that required speed. I tried a writers' group with limited success, but it was geographically undesirable, and I hadn't mastered the freeways yet.

"I need a prop," I thought. "A buddy-attracting accessory." So I had a baby.

Eureka! Motherhood was ticket for finding my people. Of course, the first tribe I entered was a mother's group, and our only common bond was that we'd all had kids between April and June of 1995, but that was good enough for me. We met, we conversed, we exchanged birthday gifts. It was a breakthrough! We're all in this together, I thought, as we shared cheese sticks and maternity clothes for baby number two. For a few years we were a tribe, until we entered the strange and sometimes lonely world of Pasadena school admissions, which tested friendships and my understanding of the importance of scissors skills.

I learned quickly that where your child ends up in school—be it private, public, parochial, or home—not only becomes your destination in the morning, but your identity, a shortcut explanation of who you are to the rest of the locals, for better or worse.

Our first attempt at admissions was a fail, as I was rejected from the co-op nursery school. Rejected! From a co-op! And I say "I" on purpose, because clearly the fault was mine, as my son screamed "co-op nursery school": unbrushed hair, mismatched clothes, pants optional. My guess is that I didn't own enough flowing skirts. So after my husband talked me down off the "he'll never get into college" ledge, I regrouped and found a perfectly sweet little nursery school where I seemed to fit in fine. Was it St. Socially Superior's or the Most Inconveniently Located but Tony Preschool? No, but it worked for us and my limited wardrobe.

All along my sons' academic trail, from preschool through high school, I found my people among the other parents, bonding over homework war stories, suffering through volunteer headaches, and leaping to conclusions about the other schools our children didn't attend. Over time, I adapted to each school's norm, becoming whatever the misconception of that school's typical parent was at the time. During the elementary years, I became blonder (but, sadly, not thinner), and I started a biweekly mani-pedi habit. By high school, I'd slapped the bumper sticker on the car, bought the mandatory baseball cap, and lapsed into the habit of asking the second most common question among parents in my area: "And where do your children go to school?" (The first, of course, is "Do you know a good SAT tutor?") Once you had the answer to the school question, you'd go straight to assuming all sorts of things about the parents without ever asking another question about jobs, interests, or favorite bands.

It was easy tribe building, if not entirely accurate.

But now my days of ready-made tribes are nearly over. Once my younger son graduates from high school, I'm on my own again. Not entirely, of course. After two decades in one place, I'm lucky to have good friends who have stuck with me, despite the fact that our kids are grown and we don't drive carpool anymore. But I'd still like to belong to a tribe, and my goal is to find one for the next phase of my life. Isn't this where I get to have more fun and less parenting? I hope so. I need some peeps who dance or craft or cook. I'm eyeing my fellow yogis in the Friday noon class; I think that group has potential. Perhaps I'll suggest a kombucha social. I'm testing the waters by volunteering for a few non-school-related organizations, and I picked up, but didn't turn in, an application to be a museum docent, an elitist tribe that appeals to my faux-academic side. Maybe we can discuss art and take a river cruise together.

And if all else fails, I'm getting another prop: a corgi.

THE GRANDMA GAP
Liz Dolan

I have a special subset of Satellite Sisters: my friends who, like me, don't have kids.

The term many use for this status is *childfree*. That kind of makes me gag. It sounds like a political position, medical condition, or a dietary restriction. You know, as in telling your waiter, "I have a nut allergy and am lactose intolerant and childfree."

Nope. I just don't have kids. When many of my friends were having their kids in their 20s, 30s, and 40s, I made other choices.

I have a *family*. Sisters and brothers, nieces and nephews—some of whom have their own kids already. I have a life that's full of family.

Not having kids of my own hasn't left a void in my life, but as I look to the future, I realize there is a gap—what I call the Grandma Gap.

Dying newsmagazines and lame morning shows love to stake out turf wars: married women vs. single woman, or working moms vs. stay-at-home moms. We've already settled this on Satellite Sisters: Do what you think is right. It's all okay. You will play many roles in your life, some of them permanently, others for a brief spell. Don't let Harvard Business School, your obstetrician, or Dr. Laura boss you around. But I digress.

Now that I am in my 50s, it's dawning on me that the biggest actual life differences are not between my single friends and my married friends, or my working friends and my stay-at-home friends. But the choices we made in those decades have an important implication for future decades. Not having kids earlier in life means we won't have grandkids later in life. And that's where the Grandma Gap comes in. I'm just peering over the edge, and the gulf between those who are parents and those who are not is starting to loom large.

I managed to be busy and fulfilled in my 30s/40s/50s without having kids, but what am I going to do in my 60s and beyond for excitement? Golf? Bunco? Bank robbery?

In our 30s and 40s, we were all so freaking busy working full time, part time, or no time; deciding about marriage, undeciding about marriage, or fighting for the right to marry; trying to have kids or not and having kids or not; changing careers or not; and moving or staying put. Plus many of us had to deal with demands from our own parents, whether it was caring about their opinions while they were living or caring for their spirits as they were dying. Yeesh. There's just a lot going on in those burning-the-candle-at both-ends years.

In the midst of all of this activity, friendships self-sort. You've got the women at work who all started in awful junior positions together. You've got the college friends you worked hard to hang onto. Mothers have some friends from school-volunteer gigs and some because their kids' playdates led to grownup friendships. And if you are me, you have the women who naturally bonded when others were rushing off to pediatrician appointments, back-to-school nights, or robotics tournaments. These friends without kids are the Satellite Sisters you text about last-minute movie dates, the ones you rent beach houses with, and the ones who know they can call your home at 11 p.m. You'll either be up watching *The Mindy Project* on your DVR or you'll be awakened by the phone and will insist you were just watching *The Mindy Project* on your DVR.

Here's where the Grandma Gap shows itself.

It's those late-night conversations that veer into the unknown territory called *What Happens Next?* Your friends with kids know (or think they know) exactly how they're going to spend their time in the third act of life, once they are no longer working so hard. They'll spend it with their kids and grandkids or grandkids-to-be. And your friends with kids know exactly who's going to take care of them when they start to fail: their kids and aforementioned grandkids or grandkids-to-be. And your friends with kids are pretty sure they know where they're going to live when they can no longer live alone. See above.

Friends with kids and grandkids (real or hoped-for) are penciling in those future birthday parties and weddings. They're projecting a pretty full dance card in later life. Their only questions are about how to fit it all in.

Meanwhile, those of us with wide-open dance cards have a lot of choices on our horizons. There's no obvious plan. And this has come as a surprise to my kid-less friends and me.

Questions among friends without kids and future grandkids run along the lines of, "Is it too late to adopt several kids and quickly put them through nursing school so they'll graduate by the time we need them to care for us?"

That plan actually starts to sound reasonable after a few margaritas.

Here's what you really talk about when you're talking to these friends about your shared fears: going broke and being helpless. Those are the two biggies. Well, actually three biggies: going broke, being helpless, and boredom. Here's how they manifest in our bad dreams:

The Bag Lady Scenario: It's amazing to me how many women I know who harbor secret fears of becoming bag ladies—broke and homeless, with no family to find them and take them in. I've even heard Oprah say she has a Bag Lady Fund set aside for herself. You'd think she be over that by now, right? Nope. Not even Oprah.

The "I've Fallen and I Can't Get Up" Scenario: When you've spent your whole adult life fending for yourself, nothing scares you more than helplessness. This fear deepens if you've spent any time caring for your own parents as they age. It's terrifying how much help they need. You can't help but wonder who's going to do that for you. Sometimes I look at my dog and wish he were Lassie. "Go! Run! Bring help, Ferris! Bark to tell them Liz is at the bottom of the well!"

The "Do You Know Who I Used to Be?" Scenario: If the first fear is financial and the second fear is physical, I guess this third one is…I don't know, sociological? Existential? You wonder what your meaning is in the world in the later stages of your life. Your identity in midlife has been largely shaped by your professional life. Once that starts to slow, what are you going to do all day? You'll have fallen into the Grandma Gap— especially if you're like me and don't play golf, belong to a church group, or garden. You are nobody's wife and nobody's mother. You've spent a lot of your life basically bossing people around. Exactly who are you going to boss around now, old lady?

These are just three of the unsettling projections you explore with your friends.

What's the fix we imagine in these conversations about the next twenty, thirty, or forty years of our lives? Honestly, I can't bear to read one more article about how I can avoid Alzheimer's if I brush my teeth with my left hand or learn a new language. I know it's my friends who are going to keep me in the game, not a book of crossword puzzles.

To accomplish this, my friends and I have decided that one thing is obvious: We need to create our own compound. I've had major conversations with friends without kids about building ourselves a small compound where we can grow old together, tended to by young, skilled people who won't be bitter about caring for us because we are not their actual parents and because they will actually be paid. These caregivers will be prohibited from ever calling us "cute" or "adorable." I hate it when people talk about old people like that. I saw how it drove my mother crazy in her later years, and I didn't blame her. No infantilizing the grownups, please. It just makes us feel more helpless.

I picture our compound as a Melrose Place kind of setup, complete with Malibu lighting, a courtyard pool for water aerobics, and an unlimited Diet Coke dispenser. We will each have our own place, but one apartment in the compound will be set aside for group dining and entertainment. And maybe a small operating theater and pharmaceutical dispensary, which we are likely to need.

This is my fantasy. I actually drive by apartment complexes near where I live in Santa Monica and think, *We could totally fix that place right up!* The fundamental difference between my imagined compound and your run-of-the-mill assisted-living center is that mine would be built on friendship and not profit margins. I'd be moving in with my friends, people I want to share my life with. It's why you have friends, after all. Growing old together is the payoff.

So, no apologies or regrets about the path not taken. I just have to spend a little more time developing a blueprint for later life than do my friends on the other side of the Grandma Gap. I won't have kids or grandkids to rely on, but you can bet that in my waning years, I'll have my friends— and a water aerobics instructor—close at hand.

The Last Word
VIRTUAL FRIENDS = REAL FRIENDS

When we started producing Satellite Sisters fifteen years ago, we had a mission to create "the sound of friendship" on the air—to capture the way real women talked when they talked to their friends. We wanted to connect with listeners by reminding them of the conversation you might have sitting around the table drinking coffee with your old college roommates or high school pals. It took us a while to find that rhythm on the air, but when we did, the listeners got it. Satellite Sisters sounded familiar, in all the best ways. And that familiarity spawned a special connection that continues to surprise us. Behind the scenes, we never anticipated how the sound of friendship on the air would translate into such a deep connection off the air with virtual friends around the globe.

After a few years of producing Satellite Sisters, the explosion of social media transformed what was once strictly a call-in relationship into a much more intimate situation. Not only did listeners get to see our pictures and the Facebook versions of our lives, but we got to see theirs. And that kind of mutually beneficial relationship we never could have predicted. Now, the Satellite Sisterhood circle was complete. You show me your Thanksgiving turkey; I'll show you mine.

It may be fashionable to dismiss virtual friendships as less than the real thing, but we've found that it's simply not true. What started as an idea cooked up by five sisters is now a living, breathing collective made up of people of all stripes connected by the idea that going through life with other people is a better way to go.

 Over the last decade or so, our virtual Satellite Sisters have shared recipes and fashion finds. They've weighed in on where to go on vacation and which sister made the best wreath. They've wished us happy birthday, merry Christmas, and happy Pancake Day. They've shared book recommendations, discussions of Oscar-worthy films, predictions on *American Idol,* and favorite Olympic moments. They've showed up at book signings, suggested fixes for our broken appliances in case our mother's patented "resting method" of repair should fail, and bought the sequined pants we tipped them off to. They've expressed their sympathy at the loss of our parents and their joy at the birth of our grandchildren.

They've laughed at our jokes, cried when we cried, and made us feel like we are part of something bigger and more worthwhile because we're going through it together.

What more could you ask for in a friend?

In turn, you've told us that we've been there for you during your divorce or your illness or your insomnia. We've helped you get through your grief, or your toughest time. We've expanded your worldview and your Netflix queue. We've reminded you of your own sisters or your daughters or your bridesmaids. We've made you laugh, we've made you cry, and we've made you feel like you're part of something bigger and more worthwhile because we're going through it together.

We're happy to be there for you.

Very often, we hear from our people that they refer to us in conversations as "my friends." As in, "My friend Sheila…" or "I heard from my friend Julie that…" When listeners reveal that, they're often sheepish, as if they'd like to have an alternative term and are looking for suggestions from us. But the truth is, "friend" is the perfect term. Because that's exactly how we think about you.

It's been a long haul. We've been through a lot together in the last fifteen years, haven't we? We're so glad you're here, friends.

Any baby yet?

Apparently never. Just me, my breathing, and my new BFF, my birthing ball.

Husband? Doula?

Asleep. Low lights & relaxation soundtrack put them out.

Oh, so that's what they mean by natural childbirth. So relaxing, everyone but mother falls asleep.

Am considering staying on this birthing ball forever. Raising child while living on ball. Possible?

Maybe you should wake one of them up.

But then I'd have to get off birthing ball. And I don't ever want to get off this ball. Ever.

I think you should definitely wake one of them up.

The Next Generation

Joining the five Dolan sisters in celebrating friendship is a cadre of young women they call the Next-Gen Sisterhood: one daughter, two daughters-in-law, and three nieces. Here's a little more about them.

Fiona Dolan is a sophomore at Summit High School in Bend, Oregon, where she lives with parents Susan and Dick Dolan (yes, the Satellite Sisters have brothers). At school, she enjoys history, writes for the newspaper, and is a starting attacker on the varsity lacrosse team. When she's not in school, she likes to be outdoors, hiking, biking, and swimming. Fiona is pretty sure her friends would describe her as loyal, adventurous, optimistic, and always ready to have a good time.

Katherine Dolan Nordenson grew up in Westport, Connecticut, with some time in São Paolo and Casablanca; her parents are Mary

McGuire and Satellite brother James Dolan. After receiving a BA in communications from Boston College, she worked in public relations for Save the Children and in digital advertising at Razorfish. Katherine is currently pursuing a master's in clinical nutrition from New York University, where she is a recipient of the 21st Century Scholarship. She's a good sport when camping, a charades enthusiast, and honored to have the loudest laugh in any group. Katherine lives in Brooklyn with her husband, Alex Nordenson.

Meghan Dolan Saporita, Katherine's big sister, is in-house counsel for a Fortune 100 insurance company. She earned a degree in English and romance literatures and languages from Harvard, went on to St. John's University School of Law, and was then named an assistant district attorney in Nassau County, New York. Meghan and her husband, Greg Saporita, are new parents who recently bought their first home in Northport, New York, directly across Long Island Sound from where she grew up in Westport. For Meghan, any day that starts with yoga and ends with TMZ is a good day.

Lauren Hinkson is an art historian in New York City who curates exhibitions of modern and contemporary art at the Guggenheim and venues abroad. A writer on topics ranging from midcentury American art to how to assemble a wedding house party, Lauren holds a degree in the history of art and architecture from Brown University, for which she mentors students through the Women's Launch Pad. She moonlights as a crafter, wedding planner, and event designer, much to her friends' delight. If you ask, she'll raise your hem, papier-mâché your bachelorette party piñata, or weave you a flower crown from the grass you are sitting on. Lauren and her husband, Julie Dolan's son William Smith, live in Brooklyn with their daughter, Josephine.

Ruthie Marantz is a Brooklyn-based filmmaker who was born and raised in New York City by her mother, Sheila Dolan. As a teenager, she produced her own public-access television show, *Rainbow Ruthie,* which ran for four years. After receiving her BA in film production from Hampshire College, she worked as line producer for *Out of Our Minds*, a selection at Sundance. She is currently an MFA candidate in NYU Tisch's graduate film program, where she is the recipient of several scholarships; Spike Lee recently awarded her the Sandra Ifraimova Production Award for her next film, *Realness.* Ruthie says her friends would describe her as "a funny girl who listens to a lot of Mariah Carey and spends all her money on food."

Vera Smith, Julie Dolan Smith's daughter-in-law, is a native of the former
Soviet country of Kyrgyzstan, a small, predominantly Muslim nation in
the mountains of Central Asia. She studied economics and international
development in Kyrgyzstan and the UK and has lived and worked in
Moscow and London. Vera now lives not far from Nana Julie in Dallas,
Texas with her husband, Nick Smith, and their three young children.
As a part of a small, women-owned firm, Vera consults with mining and
energy companies internationally on social and community issues.

Thank Yous

Many thanks to the team at Prospect Park Books, a homegrown indie press in Southern California that reminds us of ourselves in that "*Hey kids, let's put on a show!*" business model that we've embraced, too. It's a publishing company that makes it happen with a tiny staff and big ideas. Cheers to Colleen Dunn Bates and Patty O'Sullivan for their editorial insight and book-biz knowledge. Thanks to Maggie Vlahovic on the marketing and publicity front.

We love the cover and look of *You're the Best*. Many thanks to talented illustrator Nancy Nimoy, who brought the idea of a "gift to our friends" to life. And well done, book designer Amy Inouye.

We have a couple of Satellite Sisters behind the scenes who we'd like to thank for their advice, counsel, and business acumen: Yfat Reiss Gendell and her team at Foundry Literary + Media; Katie Cates at ICM; Tanya Farrell at Wunderkind PR; and Corny Koehl, executive producer at Large. Someday, a glamorous retreat at a fabulous spa for all of you on us. Until then, big hugs.

Thanks to Mary Duffy and Alan Dockery, our designers and creative team at dsquared+, who reimagined satelllitesisters.com. Additional technical and emotional support comes from Emily Tellez, who works on liandolan.com. Without you, we'd be sitting at home staring at blank screens.

Finally, lots of love and gratitude to our families. You're the best.